AT THE BEGINNING OF 2020 WE EXPERIENCED SOME OF THE WORST BUSHFIRES IN AUSTRALIAN HISTORY.

ALTHOUGH MOST OF THE COUNTRY WAS SEVERELY AFFECTED, KANGAROO ISLAND WAS AMONGST THE MOST DAMAGED.

IN AN UNPARALLELED MOVE OF KINDNESS AND SOLIDARITY, THE PEOPLE JOINED TO HELP EACH OTHER IN EVERY WAY THEY COULD.

HOWEVER AFTER ALL THE DUST HAD SETTLED, SOME WILDLIFE ORGANISATIONS WERE LEFT ON THEIR OWN TO REBUILD.

THIS IS MY PERSONAL WAY OF SAYING THANK YOU TO THOSE AMAZING PEOPLE THAT FIGHT THROUGH THE FIRE AND RAIN TO KEEP THOSE SPECIES ALIVE FOR OUR CHILDREN, EVEN WHEN WE SOMETIMES SEEM BENT ON DESTROYING THEM FOR GOOD

TO PEGGY AND MIKE:

THANK YOU FOR GIVING LEON AND
LORENZO SOMETHING TO LOOK
FORWARD.

ECHiDNA EYES

SOME PEOPLE THiNK ViCTOR CAN'T SEE WELL OR HE iS ACTUALLY BLiND.

iN FACT, ECHiDNAS HAVE GOOD EYE SiGHT, BUT SMALL EYES BECAUSE THEY ALWAYS HAVE THEiR FACE iN THE DiRT.

THEY BLiNK A LOT AND HAVE LOVELY EYELASHES THAT HELP KEEP THEiR EYES CLEAN.

ECHIDNA BELLY

ECHIDNAS DO NOT HAVE A
PERMANENT POUCH LIKE A
KANGAROO, MONOTREMES ARE
ALSO THE ONLY EGG-LAYING
MAMMALS.

TO BE A LONG TIME SURVIVOR
LAYING EGGS MAKES SENSE.

LAYING A SMALL EGG IS A LOT
LESS STRESSFUL ON MUM THAN
CARRYING AROUND AN EVERY
GROWING LITTLE ONE FOR
MONTHS ON END.

SO..... NO BELLY BUTTON

ECHIDNA TALENT

VICTOR'S SPINES ARE ACTUALLY MODIFIED HAIRS. THE ROOT GOES INTO A MUSCLE THAT ONLY ECHIDNAS HAVE. SPINES CAN BE MOVED INDIVIDUALLY SO SOME MIGHT BE LYING DOWN WHILE OTHERS STAND UP.

VICTOR CAN USE HIS SPINES LIKE FINGERS TO TURN OVER WHEN ON THEIR BACK OR TO CLIMB UP THE FORK OF A TREE.

TALK ABOUT CONTROL AND INCREDIBLY STRONG HAIRS!

VICTOR IS TRULY TALENTED!

ECHiDNA FEET

PADS ON ViCTOR'S FEET CONTAIN MECHANO RECEPTORS. THIS MEANS THEY CAN PiCK UP ViBRATiONS iN THE SOiL OR ViRTUALLY HEAR WiTH THEiR FEET, AN iNGENiOUS WAY TO FiND FOOD OR AVOiD HUMANS.

WE'RE ALSO STiLL WORKiNG ON CONViNCiNG PEOPLE THAT ViCTOR'S BACK FEET POiNT BACKWARDS.

ECHIDNA CHARACTER

ECHIDNAS HAVE GREAT
PERSONALITIES AND ARE
VERY INDIVIDUALISTIC. WHEN
ENCOUNTERING HUMANS, SOME
ARE STARTLED, SOME SHY AND
OTHERS VERY OUTGOING.

YOU WILL BE VERY HARD
PRESSED TO FIND AN GRUMPY
ECHIDNA LIKE VICTOR HERE ON A
TIMEOUT!

ECHIDNA TRAIN

ECHIDNAS ARE SOLITARY LIVING
FOR MOST OF THE YEAR.

BUT IN THE BREEDING SEASON,
MAINLY LATE JUNE THROUGH
AUGUST, ECHIDNAS FORM WHAT
IS CALLED AN ECHIDNA TRAIN.
ONE FEMALE FOLLOWED BY ANY
NUMBER OF MALES.

ECHiDNA iMPOSTOR

MANY CREATURES HAVE EVOLVED
TO GROW DiFFERENT KiNDS OF
SPiKES.

PEOPLE OFTEN WRONGLY
BELiEVE THEY ARE RELATED
TO THE EUROPEAN HEDHEHOG,
HOWEVER ViCTOR DOES NOT
HAVE:

A CUTE BUTTON NOSE
LiTTLE SHARP TEETH
EXTERNAL EAR FLAPS

ECHiDNA iMPOSTOR

MANY CREATURES HAVE EVOLVED
TO GROW DiFFERENT KiNDS OF
SPiKES.

PEOPLE OFTEN WRONGLY
BELiEVE THEY ARE RELATED
TO THE EUROPEAN HEDHEHOG,
HOWEVER ViCTOR DOES NOT
HAVE:

A CUTE BUTTON NOSE
LiTTLE SHARP TEETH
EXTERNAL EAR FLAPS

ECHiDNA SPLASH

VICTOR IS OFTEN FOUND NEAR OR IN WATER.

ALTHOUGH HE DRINKS ONLY FRESH WATER HE LOVES A GOOD SWIM IN ALL KINDS OF WATER BODIES, FROM RIVERS, TO LAKES OR EVEN THE SALTY OCEAN.

ECHIDNA BUTT

PLEASE NOTE THAT ECHIDNAS DO NOT HAVE A FLAT BUTT.

VICTOR'S REAR END FLAUNTS A MAGNIFICENT TAIL THAT BOASTS TWO PROMINENT, BEAUTIFUL SPINE ROSETTES.

JUST REMEMBER NOT TO STARE, VICTOR IS A BIT SHY

PUGGLE YOGA

ECHIDNAS AND PUGGLES LIKE VICTOR ARE TRUE CONTORTIONISTS AND CAN PRESENT THEMSELVES IN MANY SHAPES AND FORMS, FROM LONG AND ALMOST FLAT, SQUEEZED TO ROUND AND SPINY.

ECHiDNA SWiM

LiKE iTS COUSiN THE PLATYPUS, ViCTOR iS A GREAT SWiMMER. BUT HE DOESNT HAVE OR NEEDS FLiPPERS

EACH YEAR MANY ECHiDNAS LiKE ViCRTOR ARE "RESCUED" FROM THE SURF AND RETURNED TO THE BEACH, JUST TO PROMPTLY GO BACK iNTO THE SEA AGAiN.

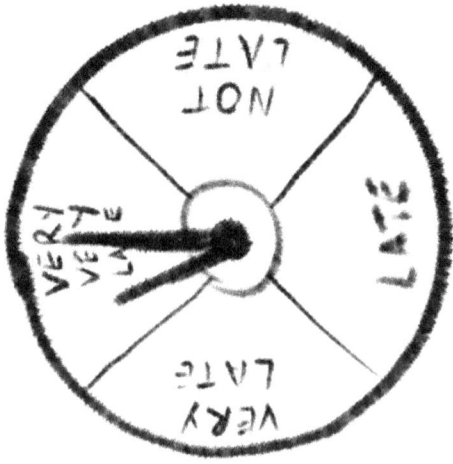

BUSY ECHDINA

IN ADDITION TO BEING JUST PLAIN DIFFERENT, ANOTHER PART OF THE ECHIDNA'S CHARISMA IS THEIR FIERCE INDEPENDENCE AND THEIR ATTITUDE.

AS A RESULT, MANY CONSERVATION, WILDLIFE CARE AND GRASS ROOTS ORGANIZATIONS HAVE ADOPTED THE ECHIDNAS LIKE VICTOR AS THEIR MASCOT.

ECHiDNA LOVE

VICTOR KNOWS WHO iS iN
CHARGE!

MANY ECHiDNAS LiKE VICTOR
FOLLOW A PRETTY GiRL FOR
WEEKS BEFORE A SiNGLE LUCKY
ONE GETS THE ENDURANCE TEST
AND A DATE.

ECHiDNA LiFE

WHAT CREATURE OUT THERE
WOULD NOT WANT TO BE AN
ECHiDNA LiKE ViCTOR?

WiTH 120 MiLLiON YEARS OF
SURVIVAL SKiLLS, THE REST OF
US MAMMAL-TYPES HAVE A
LOT OF CATCHiNG UP.

ECHIDNA CARE

ECHIDNAS ARE HUGELY ADAPTABLE AND HAVE BEEN FOUND IN EVERY TYPE OF ECOSYSTEM AROUND THE COUNTRY. BUT SADLY IN SOME AREAS THEY ARE NOW LOCALLY EXTINCT.

THEIR ANCESTORS ROAMED THE PLANET WITH THE DINOSAURS, SURVIVED ICE AGES AND NUMEROUS GLOBAL CLIMATE CHANGES. IF THE WORLD'S TOP SURVIVOR CAN'T CONTINUE IN OUR MODERN WORLD, WHAT ARE THE CHANCES FOR MERE HUMANS?